# BELLA BOUQUETS

By Alicia Schwede

Bella Bouquets
Copyright 2011
by Alicia Schwede

Library Of Congress
Cataloging-in-publication
Data Available
ISBN:978-0-615-48064-0

Design & Layout by Kimberly Schwede
www.kimberlyschwede.com

Front cover photography by Revert Photo
Back cover photographs by Karina Heneghan & Candy Apple Photography

For more information:
Flirty Fleurs Books
7711 West 6th Avenue, #D
Lakewood, CO 80214
www.flirtyfleurs.com

First Edition
Printed & Bound in China

*For my grandmother*
*who instilled the*
*deepest love of*
*flowers in me.*

*Purple garden roses,*
*lilac and pansies will*
*always hold a special*
*place in my heart.*

*I*f you've never been thrilled to the very edges of your soul by a flower in spring bloom, maybe your soul has never been in bloom.

— TERRI GUILLEMETS

# $\mathcal{C}$ONTENTS

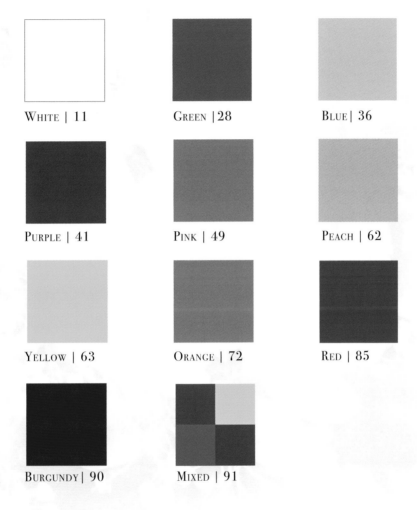

WHITE | 11

GREEN | 28

BLUE | 36

PURPLE | 41

PINK | 49

PEACH | 62

YELLOW | 63

ORANGE | 72

RED | 85

BURGUNDY | 90

MIXED | 91

PREFACE | 9

FLOWERS BY SEASON | 10

RESOURCES | 115

PHOTOGRAPHERS INDEX | 117

FLOWER INDEX | 118

# PREFACE

My devotion to flowers started at a young age, working alongside my beloved grandmother in her rose garden. We'd fill the buckets with water, grab the shears and head into the yard early in the morning when the dew was still on the grass. We'd select stems of lilac, lilies, daffodils, roses and hydrangea and place them in the buckets to hydrate. We'd select different vases & vessels and start to arrange the flowers and then place them around the house. Oh, how I love these memories. Once when I was about seven I arranged orange daylilies in a green ceramic vase and placed it on the fireplace mantle. A few hours later a neighbor came over to visit and noticed the arrangement I was so proud of and she said – "Looks like Alicia will be a florist when she grows up". Perhaps the seed was planted that day that would lead me on this path?

It seems gardens were a big part of growing up in Northern California, the flowers, berries and greens so plentiful. My mother's garden was full of shrubs with berries, interesting foliages & an array of succulents, she loves the various textures. My grandmother's neighbor, Penny, introduced me to the Garden Club. I was always amazed at how Penny could take various blooms & foliages and create the coolest vignettes for her Garden Club meetings. She grew the most beautiful flowers and how I loved clipping the fragrant sweet peas from the vines to use in my own creations. Every fall there would be a county fair with one building devoted to floral & garden designs, always the best building to whittle away the hours. The most decadent irises, garden roses, sweet peas and such all on display.

While attending college at UC Santa Barbara I would find myself visiting flower shops and stands. I was always surrounded by flowers during this period. Bougainvillea growing wild on the highway. Orchids always in bloom. I tried to get a job at a flower shop but wasn't hired on, I guess it wasn't time just yet.

I found myself working a full time job at a computer software company in San Francisco. Lunches were spent hanging out at a flower shop around the corner from the office. Soon I signed up for floral design classes at College of San Mateo. Two people from my office hired me to do their wedding flowers. I didn't fully realize it yet but the ball was rolling, my life was about to change. My boss said one day – you have a calling and you need to follow it. I did, I jumped in the deep end & opened up my first business: Alicia Chestine Designs. I surrounded myself with wonderful mentors and soaked up every bit of information I could find about floral design. Eventually my path lead me to Denver, Colorado. In March 2003 I opened Bella Fiori.

Twelve years later I still stop dead in my tracks when I spy a perfect peony, a gorgeous garden rose or sweetest sweet pea at the market. I find great pleasure in sharing my love and affection towards flowers. This book "Bella Bouquets" & the blog FlirtyFleurs.com are just a few ways for me to share & connect with others while exploring the flower path ahead.

I have dreamed of this book for many years, a place to collect my thoughts about the beautiful art of floral design. The bridal bouquet has always been one of my favorite pieces to create. Knowing that this piece will be held lovingly by a bride on her special day. A key element in the photographs in which to remember the day. I so lovingly design the bouquet, selecting the best blooms available & carefully processing each stem before it finds its special place in the bouquet. Once assembled the stems will be adorned with gorgeous ribbon. The bouquet is complete and I try to wait patiently as I anticipate handing it over to its rightful recipient.

-Alicia

# Flowers by Season

## Spring

Anemones
Daffodils
Flowering Branches
Forsythia
Frittilaria
Gardenia
Hellebores
Hyacinths
Irises
Jasmine
Lilacs
Lily of the Valley
Muscari
Narcissus
Pansies
Peonies
Poppy
Ranunculus
Tulips
Tweedia
Viburnum

## Summer

Amaranthus
Astilbe
Bachelor's Buttons
Bells Of Ireland
Clematis
Coxcomb
Cosmos
Craspedia
Dahlias
Delphinium
Garden Roses
Gladiolus
Lisianthus
Marigolds
Passion Vine
Peonies
Snapdragons
Stargazer Lilies
Stephanotis
Sunflowers
Sweet Peas
Tuberose
Tweedia
Zinnias

## Fall

Asiatic Lilies
Bittersweet
Calla Lilies
Chinese lantern
Chocolate Cosmos
Chrysanthemum
Coneflower
Coxcomb
Dahlias
Hypericum Berries
Kangaroo Paw
Maple Leaves
Montbretia
Nandina
Rosehips
Safari Sunset
Sedum
Seeded Eucalyptus
Smoke Bush
Snowberries
Solidago
Sunflowers
Viburnum Berries

## Year Round

Asiatic Lilies
Bells Of Ireland
Carnations
Freesia
Gerbera Daisies
Hydrangea
Hypericum berries
Lisianthus
Miniature Calla Lilies
Orchids
Oriental Lilies
Roses
Snapdragons
Stock

## Winter

Amaryllis
Boxwood
Camellias
Crocus
Cyclamen
Daffodils
Hellebores
Hyacinths
Ilex Berries
Kale
Muscari
Narcissus
Poinsettias
Privet Berries
Ranunculus
Star of Bethlehem

*A* romantic & timeless bouquet of gloriously scented 'Patience', 'vendela' and 'Polo' garden roses accented with Italian Ruscus.

The chic white with black center anemones wrapped with black ribbon and adorned with white pearl pins create a stylish bouquet.

Garden style design of white and green blossoms, stock fills the bouquet nicely with a lovely fragrance, bouvardia provides an interesting texture & the green tendrils from the sweetpeas adds a dainty touch of whimsy.

A delightful bouquet brimming
with blooms of white ranunculus is
surrounded by a collar of fresh
& gloriously scented mint.
The stems are completely wrapped
with a soft satin ribbon.

 $\mathcal{E}$ legant white mini-callas are combined with fragrant white freesia for a graceful bouquet wrapped with

a base of green ribbon and turquoise ribbon criss-crossing over the top.

*A* A modern style bouquet with a clutch of delicate lily of the valley placed in the center of large white calla lilies. The lilies were cut & re-constructed to create a glamelia style effect. Rolled ti leaves finish off this contemporary look.

*A* classic pairing of cream dahlias & white freesia with touches of variegated pittosporum leaves is perfect for an outdoor summer wedding.

A traditional style bouquet of 'vendela' roses is made modern with the addition of rolled ti leaves around the base of the blooms.

$\mathcal{S}$oft textures of the exoctic 'blushing bride' protea & feathery peonies finished with velvet & satin ruffled ribbon creates a luscious bouquet.

Sophisticated bouquet of all white peonies finished with white satin ribbon and rhinestone buckle charms.

Two textures are plenty when creating a stylish bouquet - 'Avalanche' roses with white Manzanita blooms make a lovely pairing.

*A*valanche' roses are combined with navy blue privet berries and finished with white & navy blue ribbons and playful blue buttons.

*Exquisite white phalaenopsis orchids create a stunning cascading bouquet.*

White gardenias, 'polo' roses and stephanotis adorned with pearls create a heavenly scented & classic all white bridal bouquet. The stems are wrapped completely with white satin ribbon & streamers of love knots are added for a sweet touch.

*A* graceful collection of all white flowers- peonies, lily of the valley, larkspur and

sweetpeas create a fabulous early summer bouquet.

A mixture of modern, rustic and elegant all wrapped into one bouquet. Significant textural interest with scabiosa pods, montbretia pods, silver dusty miller leaves, fragrant geranium leaves, poppy pods, berzillia berries and sedum are off-set by the ruffled petals of the 'patience' garden rose.

A modern cascading bouquet of mums, lisianthus, carnations & yarn balls.

*A*stylish bouquet of green Dutch hydrangea, 'super green' & 'polo' roses & white freesia

are designed in a curly willow armature. Dark brown fern fronds add an interesting touch of color

while green hanging amaranthus adds movement as the bride walks down the aisle.

Contrasting textures of voluptuous 'polo' roses with green & white variegated caladium leaves, silvery dusty miller leaves with lime green hydrangea, scabiosa pods and poppy pods are wrapped with soft lace.

*Succulents provide an understated simplicity in this modern bouquet, stems wrapped fully in white ribbon.*

A sumptuously textured bouquet of 'super green' roses, stars of Bethlehem, white sweetpeas & lisianthus, silver dusty miller leaves, green & black kangaroo paws and silver berzillia berries.

$\mathscr{B}$right & fresh 'super green' roses are rimmed with black & green kangaroo paws & wrapped

with black ribbon with a band of green ribbon in the center for a distinctive bouquet.

Sophisticated green & white lady slipper orchids create a fresh & elegant bouquet.

*G*reen trick dianthus,
white hellebores, bupleurum,
blackberries & lisianthus buds
wrapped with luxurious cream ribbon
creates a rustic yet elegant bouquet.

$\mathcal{A}$ bouquet can be created without a single bloom included. This bouquet combines a variety of textures including succulents, trick dianthus, dusty miller, loops of lily grass, brunia albiflora & berzillia berries to create a unique look.

A posy of sweet baby blue
tweedia with a touches of
velvety dusty miller leaves are
finished with a wrap
of blue polka dot ribbon.

 $\mathcal{B}$ aby blue delphiniums, purple anemones & lisianthus, are offset by chartreuse hydrangea and hanging

amaranthus. Peacock feathers add an interesting touch combining all the colors of the flowers in the bouquet.

*P*urple hyacinth blossoms
are adorned with pearl pins
& combined with dusty miller
leaves to create a
delicate posy.

𝒜petite posy of the springtime blossom muscari (grape hyacinth) finished with white ribbon and a brooch.

*A* plush bouquet of beautiful sky blue hydrangea harmonizes well with delicate white lisianthus and

freesia blooms. Finished with a rich, double-sided satin blue ribbon & silver brooch.

*A* vintage style bouquet of
'Amnesia' & 'Blue Bird' roses finished
with variegated pittosporum
leaves, stems wrapped with
cream satin ribbon.

$\mathcal{A}$ stunning & sumptuous bouquet of rich dark purple sweetpeas combined with dark plum 'Schwarzwalder' calla lilies. The stems wrapped with lavender ribbon and adorned with a strand of rhinestones.

'Schwarzwalder' calla lilies, 'sterling silver' roses, scabiosa and caladium leaves create an appealing bouquet.

Mauve hellebores, astrantia
& lilac with a touch of blue muscari
(grape hyacinth) are combined for an
unusual springtime bouquet.

The pairing of miniature calla lilies, 'blue bird' roses, sweetpeas & tulips with blackberries creates a intriguing bouquet.

*P*urple lisianthus, plum anemones, lavender tulips, blackberries & chartreuse hydrangea are enhanced with sparkling butterfly gems.

*R*ich, dark purple carnations
& a collar of rolled aspidistra leaves
creates a modern style bouquet,
dark purple ribbon with a rhinestone
buckle completes the look.

*A* mono-botanical bouquet of 'Picasso' calla lilies creates a very striking & chic bouquet, bound with eggplant hued ribbon which plays off the inner color of these lovely callas & finished with the embellishment of a decorative brooch.

$\mathscr{A}$ bridal bouquet of delicious hot pink peonies combined with hot pink calla lilies and finished with yummy scented mint & pittosporum. Bridesmaid bouquets of white peonies & calla lilies with mint & pittosporum.

*Heavenly scented 'Darcey', 'Miranda' & 'Rosalind' garden roses create a delicious mono botanical bouquet with touches of variegated pittosporum at the base.*

*Fluffy peonies & 'Yves Piaget' garden roses are accented with fuzzy chartreuse coxcomb & lamb's ear to create a splendid bouquet.*

*Garden beauties of blush pink peonies & sweet scented sweetpeas, peach ranunculus & lisianthus with Queen Anne's Lace and mint create a feminine bouquet.*

*Petite 'majolika' pink spray roses are adorned with a collar of jasmine vine and finished with embellished green ribbon.*

*D*utch 'Antique' hydrangea,
burgundy cymbidium orchids &
'panama' pink roses, pale pink
mini-calla lilies with seeded eucalyptus
interspersed throughout the bouquet.

$\mathscr{A}$ unique blend of textures from 'Yves Piaget' garden roses, nerines, ranunculus and mini-calla lilies

create an interesting monochromatic display.

$\mathcal{P}$lush pink peonies and burgundy dahlias are enhanced with harmonizing colored coleus leaves, a lovely choice for a early summer wedding.

*A*lushly designed bouquet of fuchsia cattleya orchids, deliciously scented 'Yves Piaget' garden roses,

elegantly draping phalaenopsis orchids, delicate sweet peas with touches of green mint to complement

the myriad of hot pink tones. Rhinestone butterflies add a touch of bling to this opulent bouquet.

A pleasing garden style bouquet of pink dahlias, 'topaz' & 'sweet unique' roses, 'hot pink folies' spray roses are contrasted nicely with the green bells of Ireland & hypericum berries.

$\mathcal{A}$ unique & textured bouquet of
coxcomb, carnations, saracena lilies,
peonies and glorisa lilies are
bejeweled with pink flower gems.
The stems are wrapped with
fun beaded wire.

*A*ll pink dahlias create a distinct & stylish bouquet with a brooch embellishment on the stems wrapped in pink satin ribbon.

*A* feminine collection of blush & rosy pink peonies & cyclamen accented with silvery dusty miller.

*A* opulent bouquet of 'Juliet'
garden roses, peach spray roses,
ranunculus & sweetpeas surrounded
by pieris japonica (andromeda).

Combining the traditional carnation with the adored golden ranunculus & adding in velvety dusty miller leaves creates a vintage style bouquet.

'Pot of Gold' mini-callas are surrounded by cheerful yellow freesia and loops of green & white variegated lily grass. The stems are wrapped with green satin ribbon & fun green beads.

A textured blend of yellow dahlias, golden pincushion proteas, green hypericum berries, chocolate cosmos, sunflowers with their yellow petals removed & rolled croton leaves create an interesting & unusual bouquet.

The hip craspedia (Billy Balls) is encircled by dainty kamille flowers creating a rustic yet modern bouquet. Bands of raffia on the stems play up the rustic theme.

*Y*ellow football Chrysanthemums (Mums) are once again becoming popular. Here they are shown in a fashionable & contemporary bouquet adorned with turquoise & yellow ribbons.

*A* robust hand-tied bouquet of yellow pincushion proteas (Leucospermum), craspedia ( billy balls), succulents & rolled aspidistra leaves.

Springtime collection of yellow acacia, craspedia (Billy Balls), tulips, and daffodils accented with pink sweetpeas makes for a vivacious display.

Contrasting intricate textures are combined in this bouquet of yellow kangaroo paws, craspedia (Billy Balls), acacia, spray roses and delicate peach ranunculus.

$\mathcal{B}$rilliant yellow mini-callas are surrounded by the modern ball-shaped craspedia (billy balls) for a chic bouquet.

Wrapped with a slate gray ribbon & accented with black pins creates a crisp, modern style.

Peach finess' & orange 'milva' roses combined with like colored rosehips form the perfect look for a late summer wedding.

*S*leek & simple mango miniature calla lilies can produce a chic bouquet bound in just two places with gold beads.

*A* robust bouquet of red dahlias, orange ranunculus, chocolate cosmos, coreopsis, 'black beauty', 'orange unique' & 'circus' roses works wonderfully for a late summer or early fall wedding.

*A* rustic fall bouquet
of scabiosa pods, euphorbia,
'orange unique', 'circus',
'freedom' & ' skyline' roses.

*A* classic fall bouquet of two-toned 'circus', red 'freedom', yellow 'gold strike', orange 'milva' & 'orange unique' roses.

For the bride that wants to make a
bold statement, orange tulips rimmed
with orange & gold coxcomb and
wrapped with gold wire and beads.

*M*ango miniature calla lilies are accented with fern fronds

and have a collar of glossy green galax leaves.

A vivacious fall bouquet of
light orange spider gerbera daisies,
orange gerbera daisies, 'circus' roses,
yellow miniature calla lilies,
hypericum berries and
nandina leaves.

*A* colorful & spunky bouquet of red spider gerbera daisies, 'schwarzwalder' miniature calla lilies,

craspedia (Billy Balls), orange with red tip dahlias and French parrot tulips.

*T*wo-toned 'circus', 'orange unique', red 'freedom, yellow 'gold strike' roses, orange 'mambo' spray roses, burgundy dahlias & mango miniature calla lilies are accented with green hanging amaranthus.

*A* fall bouquet of all berries – privet, Manzanita, madrone, pyracantha & seeded eucalyptus.

*Tinted orange sunflowers wrapped with raffia create a fresh rustic look for a fall wedding.*

*A* nosegay of rusty orange
cymbidium orchids create
a sophisticated look for a
fall wedding.

*A* twist on the traditional red rose bouquet. By combining the three shapes & hues of the red 'Hearts' roses, 'rubicon'& 'Scarlette' spray roses depth is nicely conveyed in the bouquet. Finished with a wrap of cream ribbon and a fun red tassel for movement.

Exquisitely formed red parrot
tulips gathered en masse create
a ravishing bouquet. A fabulous
bouquet when tulips are in their
prime blooming months during
the winter & spring.

*Harmonizing tones of red & burgundy dahlias paired with 'hearts' red roses and accented with navy blue privet berries create a rich jewel toned bouquet, perfect for a bride that wants to make a dramatic statement.*

*A* engaging bouquet of ruffly
red ranunculus & scarlet anemones
with intriguing dark centers bound
with a rich red silk ribbon.

$\mathcal{A}$ red monochromatic bouquet full of textures, 'hearts' & 'forever young' roses, 'mokara red' orchids,

gerbera daisies & tulips are finished with a collar of rolled red ti leaves. The stems are wrapped with lace

from the bride's mother's dress on top of red ribbon.

*A* sensual bouquet of
burgundy dahlias, hellebores,
dusty miller and flowering
thyme creates a vintage feel.

*A* delightful cascading bouquet brimming with spring blossoms– pink & white parrot tulips, pink cymbidium orchids, lavender, lavender sweet peas, pink miniature calla lilies & hot pink hydrangea.

*A* unique fall color palette of antique turquoise & green hydrangea, velvety burgundy dahlias, whimsical fern fronds, burgundy miniature calla lilies and added texture with burgundy sedum.

$\mathcal{A}$ lavish hand-tied bouquet of 'Ken Donson' clematis and plush pink & blush garden roses with caladium & geranium leaves.

*Y*ellow & red
French parrot tulips,
red spider gerbera daisies &
yellow craspedia (billy balls)
combine for a captivating bouquet.

The yellow edges of the hot pink gloriosa lilies are emphasized by the yellow of the 'Pot of Gold' miniature calla lilies creating a cheerful & contemporary bouquet

*A* romantic collection of delicate blush ranunculus, 'Juliet' garden roses, ruffly dahlias, sweet baby blue tweedia, fragrant mint & geranium leaves, scabiosa pods for a bit of textural interest and soft gray lamb'sear.

$\mathcal{A}$ bridal bouquet of anemones, fluffy peonies & 'polo' roses. Bridesmaids bouquets are comprised of colorful

blooms of lilac, anemones, sweetpeas and 'Juliet' garden roses.

$\mathscr{A}$ lavish jewel toned bouquet of the bi-color red & white 'crazy one' roses, velvety burgundy dahlias, plum anemones,

sweetly scented indigo hyacinths, light blue delphinium & plum ranunculus.

*W*hite sweetheart roses are embellished with rhinestones and nestled inside Schwarzwalder᾽ miniature calla lilies

& accented with black feathers to create a sophisticated bouquet.

_S_pring mix of peach ranunculus,
gold spray roses, Icelandic poppies,
'sangria' dahlias & yellow
oncidium orchids.

$\mathcal{A}$ hip bouquet of mango
miniature calla lilies are surrounded
by bright pink 'sweet unique' roses
and touches of dark green
pittosporum leaves.

*K*ermit mums (chrysanthemums) placed in the center of hot pink gerbera daisies for a playful touch. Pearls add a bit of bling & secure the mums in place.

A splendid garden style bouquet of magenta peonies, hot pink nerines, chartreuse fuji spider mums & 'super green' roses. Jasmine vine twines around the bouquet for added interest.

$\mathscr{A}$ collection of bridesmaids' bouquets, fall inspired bouquets of antique green hydrangea, red dahlias, orange ranunculus, 'circus' roses and touches of seeded eucalyptus.

*A* luscious pairing of dark purple antique hydrangea, 'Juliet' roses, navy blue privet berries and touches of fancy fern.

*A* garden style bouquet of pale pink 'Sophie' roses, white freesia, lisianthus, sweetpeas, hydrangea & arabicum. Sweet smelling mint & seeded eucalyptus add to the lushness of the bouquet.

A brightly hued bouquet perfect for an outdoor summer celebration. A hand-tied bouquet of luscious magenta peonies, 'orange unique' roses, orange ranunculus, lime green with pink centered cymbidium orchids, green hypericum berries & the intriguing fern frond.

A early spring inspired bouquet of pale yellow ranunculus & double tulips combined with delicate grape hyacinths (muscari), trick dianthus, lady's mantle and soft silver dusty miller. Wrapped with a yellowgreen ribbon to play off the colors of the tulips & ranunculus.

A late spring garden inspired bouquet of the lovely 'Juliet' garden roses, fragrant lilac, purple anemones, plum ranunculus accented with bright green trick dianthus, lisianthus buds add a bit of whimsy.

*R*ed & yellow stripped tulips wrapped with red polka dot ribbon for a fun & flirty look.

*A* hand-tied bouquet of
lovely red, orange, gold &
magenta ranunculus.

*For more inspiration please visit:*
www.bellafiori.com

# ESOURCES

AMATO WHOLESALE FLORIST, INC.
6601 Downing Street
Denver CO 80229
www.amatodenver.com
Fresh cut flowers & hard goods

M&J FABRICS
1008 Avenue of the Americas
New York, NY 10018-5402
www.mjtrim.com
Ribbons, buttons and trims

CHALK HILL CLEMATIS
P.O. Box 1847
Healdsburg, CA 95448
www.chalkhillclematis.com
Large selection of cut clematis

PUNA KAMALII FLOWERS INC.
16-211 Kalara St.
Keaau, HI 96749
www.punakamaliiflowers.com
866-982-8322
Large selection of fresh orchids

FLORAL SUPPLY SYNDICATE
Stores Nationwide
www.fss.com
Ribbons & bouquet accents

STEVENS AND SON WHOLESALE
FLORIST
14022 W. 54th Avenue
Arvada, Co. 80002-1516
www. stevensandson.com
Fresh cut flowers

JO ANN FABRICS & CRAFTS
Stores Nationwide
www.joann.com
1-888-739-4120
Ribbons, buttons & fabrics

*Happiness is to hold flowers in both hands."*
– JAPANESE PROVERB

# INDEX OF PHOTOGRAPHERS

Adam & Imthiaz Photographers (www.ahpphotos.com), 13, 106

Andrea Flanagan Photography (www.andreaflanagan.com), 16

Andrew & Jessica Photographers (www.andrewandjessica.com), 52, 92, 93

Apex Images (www.apeximages.com), 28, 89

Autumn Burke Photography (www.autumnburke.com), 20, 26, 45, 47, 62, 69, 85, 86, 87, 105

Candy Apple Photography (www.candyapplephotography.com), 57

Cooley Photography (www.cooleyphoto.com), 81

Dave Russell Photography (www. daverussellphotography.com), 49

Jamee Photography (www.jameephotography.com), 97

Jared Wilson Photography (www.jaredwilsonphotography.com), 37, 53, 65, 108

Jensen Sutta Photography (www.jensensutta.com), 80

Karina Heneghan Photographics (www.karinaheneghan.com), 2, 109

Keri Doolittle Photography (www.keridoolittlephotography.com), 27

Kern Photo (www.kern-photo.com), 25

Revert Photo (www.revertphoto.com), 68, 91, 112, 113

This Modern Life Photography (www.thismodernlifephoto.com), 71

*A special thank you to the photographers who provided us with amazing photographs of our designs which are displayed throughout this book.*

# $\mathcal{I}$NDEX OF FLOWERS

Acacia, 69, 70

Amaranthus, 28, 37, 81

Amaryllis, 102

Anemones, 12, 37, 46, 88, 98, 99, 111

Arabicum, 108

Aspidistra, 68

Astrantia, 44

Bells of Ireland, 58

Berzillia berries, 26, 31, 35

Billy balls, 66, 68, 69, 70, 71, 80, 95

Blackberries, 34, 45, 46

Blushing bride protea, 19

Bouvardia, 13

Brunia, 35

Bupleurum, 34

Caladium leaves, 29, 43, 94

Calla lilies, 16

Carnations, 27, 47, 59, 63

Cattleya orchids, 57

Chocolate cosmos, 65, 74

Chrysanthemums, 27, 67, 104, 105

Clematis, 94

Coleus leaves, 56

Coreopsis, 74

Coxcomb, 51, 59, 77

Craspedia, 66, 68, 69, 70, 71, 80, 95

Croton leaves, 65

Curly Willow, 28

Cyclamen, 61

Cymbidium orchids, 54, 84, 91, 109

Daffodils, 69

Dahlias, 17, 56, 58, 60, 65, 74, 80, 87, 90, 92, 93, 97, 99, 101, 106

Delphinium, 37, 99

Dusty miller, 26, 29, 31, 35, 36, 38, 61, 63, 90, 110

Euphorbia, 75

Fern fronds, 28, 78, 92, 93, 109

Freesia, 15, 17, 28, 40, 64, 108

Galax leaves, 78

Garden Roses, 11, 26, 50, 51, 55, 57, 62, 94, 97, 98, 107, 111

Gardenias, 24

Gerbera daisies, 79, 89, 104

Glorisa lilies, 59, 96

Grape hyacinth, 39, 44, 110

Hellebores, 34, 44, 90

Hyacinth, 38, 99

Hydrangea, 28, 29, 37, 40, 46, 54, 91, 92, 93, 106, 107, 108

Hypericum berries, 28, 58, 65, 79, 109

Jasmine, 53, 105

Kamille, 66

Kangaroo paws, 31, 32, 70

Lady slipper orchids, 33

Lady's mantle, 110

Lamb's ear, 51, 97

Larkspur, 25

Lavender, 91

Lilac, 44, 98, 111

Lily grass, 35, 64

Lily of the Valley, 16, 25

Lisianthus, 27, 31, 34, 37, 40, 46, 52, 108, 111

Miniature calla lilies, 15, 42, 43, 45, 48, 49, 54, 55, 64, 71, 73, 78, 79, 80, 81, 91, 92, 93, 96, 100, 103

Mint, 14, 49, 52, 57, 97, 108

Mokara orchids, 89

Montbretia pods, 26

Mums, 67, 104, 105

Muscari, 39, 44, 110

Nandina, 79

Nerines, 55, 105

Oncidium orchids, 101

Peonies, 19, 20, 25, 49, 51, 52, 56, 59, 61, 98, 105, 109

Phalaenopsis orchids, 23, 57

Pieris japonica, 62

Pincushion protea, 65, 68

Poppies, 101

Poppy pods, 26, 29

Privet berries, 22, 82, 87, 107

Queen anne's lace, 52

Ranunculus, 14, 52, 55, 62, 63, 70, 74, 88, 97, 99, 101, 106, 109, 110, 111, 113

Rosehips, 72

Roses, 11, 18, 21, 22, 24, 28, 29, 31, 32, 41, 43, 45, 53, 54, 58, 72, 74, 75, 76, 79, 81, 85, 87, 89, 98, 99, 102, 103, 105, 106, 108, 109

Saracena lilies, 59

Scabiosa, 43

Scabiosa pods, 26, 29, 75, 97

Sedum, 26, 92, 93

Seeded eucalyptus, 54, 82, 102, 106, 108

Spider gerber daisies, 79, 80, 95

Spray roses, 53, 58, 62, 70, 81, 85, 100, 101

Stars of Bethlehem, 31

Stephanotis, 24

Stock, 12

Succulents, 30, 35, 68

Sunflowers, 65, 83

Sweet peas, 13, 25, 31, 42, 45, 52, 57, 62, 69, 91, 98, 108

Trick dianthus, 34, 35, 110, 111

Tulips, 45, 46, 69, 77, 80, 86, 89, 91, 95, 110, 112

Tweedia, 36, 97